Copyright details

Published by Wood Wide Web Education (ABN: 25 745 636 312)

Previous versions of this content were published online as the series "Australian Bush Tucker Bites" in *The Daily Cuppa*. The author would like to thank publication owner and editor, Katie Michaelson, for her support in creating this work and developing it into this new form.

The following images were used in accordance with the conditions of use outlined on Canva.com for Canva Pro Subscribers.

Page 16 - Chocolate Lily - Andrew Haysom

ISBN: 978-0-6457141-1-1

A catalogue record for this book is available from the National Library of Australia

Acknowledgement of Country

I would like to acknowledge the traditional custodians of
the land and their contribution to caring for
Australia's unique habitats, ecosystems and
biomes for thousands of years.
I would like to thank the Wangerriburra
people of South East Queensland and the Gulgnay
people of Far North Queensland whose countries
I have been fortunate to explore and nurture.
I pay respect to the elders past, present
and emerging who maintain precious wisdom
and knowledge about our natural environment.
Exploration of bush tucker would not be as rich if
it weren't for the custodianship of the
traditional owners of the land.

Magpie Lark

IMPORTANT

Disclaimer

Olive-backed Sunbird

While every effort has been made to ensure the accuracy
of the information in this ebook, content is for
entertainment purposes only. **It is not intended as a
guide to identify wild plants**, but could be used to
populate your garden with new species from trusted
suppliers.
Readers should not consume anything without
conducting their own research and ensuring correct
identification of living things. Readers should also take
care when trying new foods for the first time as
previously unknown intolerances may become apparent.

What is this Bush Tucker you speak of?

"Bush Tucker" is so pervasive in Australian vernacular that it never occurred to me that it was a singularly Australian term. This became obvious when I started writing a series of articles on medium.com for a publication called *The Daily Cuppa*.

"Bush Tucker" is used to describe Australian native plants, animals and insects that First Nations people used to sustain their lifestyles before colonisation.

In fact, many of the early European explorers and settlers also consumed bush tucker before European species were introduced to the continent.

There's a general and incorrect assumption by many Australians that this sunburned country was barren, but a little research reveals that healthy and tasty bush tucker is everywhere if you only know where to look for it. Recent archaeological evidence also supports the contention that First Nations people had sustained agricultural and cultivation practices for thousands, if not tens of thousands of years before Australia was colonised.

An important component of traditional wisdom that has accompanied the use of bush tucker plants is the concept of reciprocity. We must not just take from bush tucker plants without giving back to them. We can do this by including them in our gardens and caring for them and the soil around them. We should only harvest what we need and leave enough for others, humans and wildlife, to harvest.

In this book the focus is on a sample of the flora and two of the insects that sustained the First Nations Peoples of Australia and how bush tucker is used today.

The accompanying hope is that, with awareness, more of these plants will be nurtured in gardens and parks and bush rehabilitation projects helping maintain ecosystems that support this amazing country. By creating a demand for these species, we will also encourage industry to supply them.

1

Read on for culinary delights and medicinal marvels!

Alexandra Palm

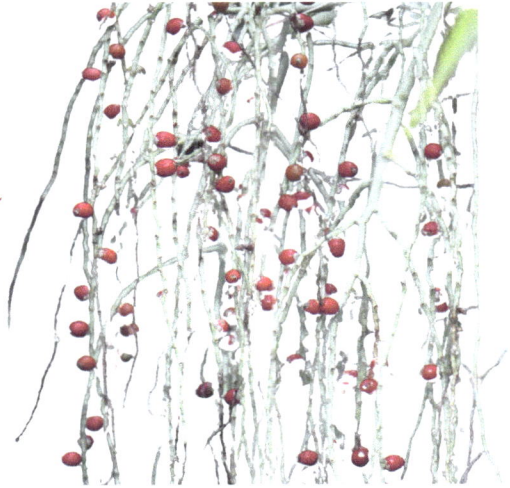

Alexandra Palm
(*Archontophoenix alexandrae*)

Eat your heart out with this tropical palm!

Just make sure you've got the right palm. This plant is a good example why scientific names are a must. There are a number of palms with similar common names.

This palm grows in north-eastern Australia. Its amazing adaptations allow it to tolerate inundation and cyclonic winds.

It is also useful to plant along streams and riverbanks as its roots bind the soil together and prevent erosion.

The Girringun people of the Cassowary Coast in North Queensland have used it for thousands of years and call it *Gubungara*. They chop down the palm and carve out the growing heart to eat.

The seeds were used to make necklaces while the sheaths from the base of leaves were used to carry honey or water.

The timber was used to make spear points and the leaves were woven into baskets.

The fruit is also edible when cooked as are the leaf bases.

It seems that no part of the plant was wasted.
A truly sustainable harvest!

2

Aniseed Myrtle

Aniseed Myrtle
(*Syzygium anisatum*)

Oh, the delicious smell of these crushed leaves!

Aniseed or Anise Myrtle is a fussy rainforest plant and susceptible to Myrtle Rust, but totally worth the effort!

Traditionally used to calm the stomach by First Nations people, it is now becoming popular amongst chefs experimenting with native Australian foods.

There has been little research on this plant but initial studies suggest a nutrient profile similar to Lemon Myrtle. It also contains the compound anethole which supports claims of its efficacy in treating intestinal conditions.

During World War Two, aniseed flavours became difficult to source and it has been reported that Aniseed Myrtle leaves were used to make an energising tonic for soldiers, amongst other culinary applications in Australian kitchens.

The leaves are high in mineral content (including Magnesium, Zinc and Calcium) and has anti-microbial properties.

Infuse fresh leaves for a delicious aniseed tea or dry and powder the leaves to flavour sweet and savoury dishes! You can also use it as a substitute for Star Anise.

The essential oil has also been shown to attract fish to lures!

3

Atherton Raspberry
(*Rubus probus*)

A raspberry that thrives in warm climates!

This species (one of eight species native to Australia) grows happily in warm climates right up to the tropics, unlike its exotic cousins that prefer cooler weather over winter.

The fruits are large and succulent. Established plants have been reported to yield as much as 3 kilograms (6.6 pounds) of fruit per plant! It typically fruits in Summer and Autumn, but can also fruit sporadically throughout the year.

First Nations people also reportedly ate the new shoots and leaves. Pregnant women are advised to avoid drinking the leaf tea from this plant as it may result in miscarriage.

This species is starting to be grown commercially in Australia, but the industry is in its infancy.

There's a trick to harvesting the fruits. Red doesn't necessarily mean ripe. In the last 24 hours of development, the fruit almost doubles in size and then it falls into the hand at the slightest touch. If you have to "pick" it, it's not ready.

Atherton Raspberries can be eaten fresh from the garden or used in the kitchen like other *Rubus* species, for

- jams
- jellies
- pies, and
- pastries.

Available in the United States as the cultivar Raspberry "Queensland".

Australian Gardenia

Australian Gardenia
(*Attractocarpus fitzalanii*)

Huge lush, waxy, deep green leaves, light green delicate new growth, lusciously scented blooms and tangy yellow fruit. What more could you ask for?

Australian Gardenia was prized and harvested by First Nations people for thousands of years before Australia was colonised.

Despite being grown as a street tree in many North Queensland towns, most Australians don't know about it and research has yielded no information about its nutritional profile.

In landscaping it is suitable for containers, hedges or as a small shade tree, providing it is pruned to purpose.

It can be dioecious, meaning that it has male and female plants, or monoecious. Outside its tropical home, authorities recommend only growing male trees as birds love the fruit and spread the seed which germinates readily.

Fruit can be eaten fresh when ripe and is similar to Asia's popular Mangosteen and sometimes this tree is even called Yellow Mangosteen.

Fruits may also be used in various dishes like:
- salads
- tarts
- custards
- cakes, and
- snack balls.

Blue Quandong

Blue Quandong
(*Elaeocarpus species*)

You'll have to beat the dinosaurs to the forest floor to sample this one!

Blue is rare in nature but in the rainforests of Far North Queensland, there is a blue fruit that scatters across the forest floor like a spilled dragon's hoard of sapphires. You probably won't find any dragons nearby but you might find a dinosaur!

The Southern Cassowary looks like a dinosaur, has fearsome claws and loves to eat Blue Quandongs. It is generally accepted that Cassowaries have helped the species spread through the region and that seed germination is improved by travelling through their digestive tract.

The people from the Girringun language group of the "Cassowary Coast" called this tree *Murrgan* and peeled the thin blue skin from the fruit to reveal a thin layer of flesh over a large seed. This flesh was washed off the seed in water before consumption.

While usually found on the forest floor, fruit can also be picked from the tree for consumption providing that it is completely blue indicating ripeness.

There is little nutritional information available for this sour fruit with more attention being given to its distant southern cousin also called Quandong.

6

Blue Tongue Plant
(*Melastoma affine*).

Forget blue tongue lollies, these berries will give children the blue tongue while they eat fruit!

Oh the joy from this plant! Not only does it have beautiful flowers and edible fruits, it attracts a plethora of native bees. It's my first recommendation to people wanting a bush tucker garden that attracts bees.

It is called the Blue Tongue Plant because the ripe berries give one a blue tongue. Children love them! Taste-wise they are a little bland, but it's the tongue colour that attracts them.

In good conditions it flowers and fruits all year. Blue Tongue plant prefers part shade and regular watering, as well as a prune every so often.

This marginal rainforest plant is native to tropical Australia and up through Asia to India. It has recently been reclassified as *Melastoma malabithricum.*

In Malaysia, it is a part of herbal lore, claiming to treat conditions such as dysentery, toothache, cuts, wounds, and diarrhea amongst others.

The First Nations people of Far North Queensland used leaves and petals medicinally as well as eating the soft berries.

Young leaves and shoots can be eaten cooked or raw and have a pleasant sourness, according to Singaporean anecdotes.

When cooked the berries sweeten without losing their vibrant hue making them perfect for baking in muffins, tarts, biscuits and more!

Bolwarra
(*Eupomatia laurina*)

Copper leaves and flowers from Gondwana.

This tree is a survivor from the first flowering plants to appear on the supercontinent Gondwana. With flowers reliant on weevils from the *Elleschodes* genus for pollination, it is like many "primitive" plants that haven't adapted to a variety of pollinators. This also threatens its survival. If something should happen to the weevils, Bolwarra may disappear over time.

The fruits are reminiscent of guava and are also known as Native Guava or Copper Laurel which refers to the colour of older leaves in Winter and Spring.

Bolwarra is the name given to the tree by Australia's original inhabitants and references tens of thousands of years of its use as a food by First Nations people.

Bolwarra fruit ripens in Winter slowly turning from green to brown. When completely brown and soft fruits can be eaten fresh or used in drinks, jams and jellies as a spice fruit.

It can also be dried and powdered and used as a spice.

If nothing else, it can be grown for the sweet-smelling flowers in Summer and gorgeous foliage all year long.

Brahmi
(*Bacopa monnieri*)

A tiny aquatic herb with a rich medicinal history.

Found in both freshwater and brackish wetlands in coastal areas, its endemic range is controversial. Some sources list it as native to Australia while others say it has naturalised after introduction. Regardless, it is a useful plant to have around.

This herb may be more familiar to you as
- Water Hyssop
- Memory Herb
- Thyme-leaf Gratiola
- Indian Pennywort, or
- Herb of Grace.

A staple in Ayurvedic medicine, it has been used medicinally for thousands of years in India. It is renowned for its health benefits and is commonly consumed to improve memory and longevity. It has also been used to treat anxiety and mental fatigue.

It can be eaten raw in salads or cooked as a vegetable in soups and stirfries.

It's a lovely edible to keep in a pond and is also fully submersible in an aquarium.

Brisbane Wattle
(*Acacia fimbriata*)

Nutrition, ecosystem services and golden blooms! What's not to love?

The striking golden blooms of this small tree line the roads in its native range in late Winter and early Spring. It's a delightful addition to any garden just for that!

Following the blooms, the trees are bedecked with pods that start green and slowly turn brown. These seeds are edible and loved by native birds.

Wattleseed from this and other species is becoming commercially available, but difficulty in efficiently harvesting the seeds keeps demand greater than supply.

First Nations people harvested the seeds and ate them raw or roasted and pounded them using strong bark and rocks to make a gluten-free flour that is prized today.

The roasted seeds have a pleasant nutty flavour that can also be used to season meats or make pastry.

The seeds are also wonderfully nutritious, containing:
- up to 20% protein
- potassium
- fibre
- unsaturated fats and oils, and
- starchy carbohydrates.

10

Burdekin Plum
(Pleiogynium timorense)

Pick the plums and bury them in soil to ripen!

No, really!

This is how First Nations people encouraged the fruit to ripen, lose their hardness and soften the acidity. At the first signs of ripening they would pick and then bury the fruit in sandy soil for at least a few days before consumption.

The Girringun People of the "Cassowary Coast" called this tree, *Ngaguba* and cultivate the different varieties for bush rehabilitation projects. There are two varieties, one with green/white flesh and the more tart and better known variety sporting bright red flesh.

The red fruit is gorgeous, a deep purple-red when ripe. Burdekin Plum is also known as Tulip Plum referencing its unique shape.

With five times the antioxidant content of blueberries plus vitamin C, the plums are full of nutrition.

If you can get your hands on some, you can use them in a number of ways:
- fruit salads
- jams
- chutneys
- pies and crumbles (rhubarb substitute)
- ferment into wine, or
- cook them down and use them to make gravy for game meats such as kangaroo or emu.

11

Bush Basil

Bush Basil
(*Coleus graveolens*)

Add this Australian herb from the mint family to your Mediterranean dishes!

Bush Basil was called Five-Spice Plant by Australian colonists, referencing its blend of sage, oregano, basil and mint, as well as its similarity to *Plectranthus amboinicus* or Five Spice Plant. Until recent reclassification it was known as *Plectranthus graveolens.*

For thousands of years, First Nations people used it as a ceremonial herb and medicinal herb for ailments like coughs and colds. It can be made into a tea by simply steeping the fresh leaves in water.

Other modern uses include scattering fresh new leaves on pizza, pasta, or salads. It is also combined with pine nuts to make pesto. Indeed, it can be used as a substitute for fresh Basil in most dishes. It should be used sparingly as it is much more pungent. The flowers are also edible.

This versatile herb can also be dried, and loses some of its pungent intensity in the process.

Some sources claim it as a possum deterrent excellent for border and spot planting in vegetable patches. Another reason to love it s for the wonderful pollinators that crowd around the purple flower spikes!

12

Chocolate Lily

Chocolate Lily
(*Arthropodium fimbriatum*)

An Australian Easter alternative full of chocolatey goodness.

The flowers of this plant release a delicious chocolate aroma with notes of vanilla and caramel into the air. They flower from September to January and must have been delightful prior to decline due to the introduction of grazing sheep by colonial settlements when they occupied entire meadows.

This stunning lily is found in grasslands and woods in temperate regions to the subtropics, with a preference for cooler, dryer climates.

The edible flower can be used in salads or desserts, but it's the tuber that sustained First Nations people in pre-colonial Australia. It was amongst many tubers that were cultivated in an organised agricultural system that some sources argue has partly domesticated this plant.

The Dja Dja Wurrung People of Central Victoria called this plant *Gitjawil matom.*

The tuber is reportedly best eaten lightly roasted with butter to enjoy the juicy, sweet and bitter flavours. Some sources say they taste like hot chips!

Cinnamon Myrtle
(*Backhousia myrtifolia*)

Bush Cinnamon with notes of pepper and nutmeg!

This is popular as a hedge, screen or windbreak with its lush green growth, compact habit and creamy star-shaped flowers. It's also relatively drought tolerant once established.

First Nations people used it medicinally as an anti-inflammatory and to treat digestive complaints. It also has anti-bacterial and anti-fungal properties.

It has many different common names including Grey Myrtle, Neverbreak and Ironwood, referencing its hardwood qualities.

Endemic to the subtropical forests of Southern Queensland and Northern New South Wales, the strong pink/grey timber was used for furniture and tool handles.

The leaves can be infused to make herbal tea or, if dried and ground, make a perfect Cinnamon substitute to use in:

- baked goods
- curries
- stews
- Middle-Eastern recipes, and
- mulled wine.

If you choose to experiment with this one though, start small as it tends to be more intense than traditional cinnamon varieties.

Coastal
Saltbush

Coastal Saltbush
(Atriplex cinerea)

Pass the Salt Bush Please!

If the gorgeous silver-green foliage isn't enough for you, this plant has leaves that can be dried and used as a salt substitute.

The leaves are also used in stuffings, marinades, stir-fries or simply blanched and boiled as a salty spinach substitute.

First Nations people ate the leaves and also crushed the leaves in water to treat skin abrasions.

These plants were also a key component in the agricultural practices of First Nations people. They were used as windbreaks, firebreaks and to rehabilitate soils with high salinity.

It's useful for modern-day agriculture for the same reasons, as well as providing fodder for stock animals.

These plants are also recommended to stabilise soil on dunes, roadsides and firebreaks. The silvery leaves reflect light and provide extra visibility at night if Coastal Saltbush is used along the verges of roads or driveways.

You'll find Coastal Saltbush in exposed positions with saline soil along most of the Australian coastline.

Partner it up with Pepperberry and you've got some all-Aussie seasoning for your tucker!

Creeping Boobialla
(*Myoporum parvifolium*)

Berries from a sun-loving groundcover!

This lush green groundcover features white or pink flowers that develop into yellow-green berries that ripen to purple.

Most sources state that the fully ripe berries are edible, but some sources disagree.

This was a traditional bush food for First Nations people but the name is the result of miscommunication. *Bubiala* was the name First Nations people in Tasmania gave to an Acacia species, but has now become the name for plants in the genus Myoporum when colonists misunderstood which plant was being discussed.

The fruits range from sweet to bitter depending on growing conditions and climate. Another common name given to species in this genus is Native Juniper.

Creeping Boobialla is a species most commonly found on limestone cliffs in South Australia and Western Victoria. In good conditions, it produces a thick green mat which flowers profusely with white or pink flowers.

These days, Creeping Boobialla is most often found in landscaped gardens, falling over rockery edges and covering the ground in sunny areas. Some sources list it as an excellent garden plant for fire-prone areas due to its resistance to flame.

Curry Myrtle

Curry Myrtle
(*Backhousia angustifolia*)

The subtropical rainforest in Eastern Australia hosts a plant that makes delicious bush curry.

This gem prefers a shaded position alongside a waterway in subtropical dry rainforests.

Crushing the foliage releases the most delicious curry smell with a hint of bush honey. Apparently, the flavour varies based on environmental conditions in the immediat area and can include aniseed and rosemary.

It's hard to find in the wild because dry rainforests are being cleared at a rapid rate to expand agriculture and build houses.

There has been little research done on this obscure plant, but it is thought to have antioxidant and antifungal properties similar to other *Backhousia* species.

It makes a lovely bushy garden feature or screening plant that can grow to seven metres, but is still dense to the ground.

The dried leaves can be crumbled to use in
- meat rubs
- breads, or
- to make a bush laksa.

Plant one today and help save the species!

Finger Lime
(*Citrus australisica*)

Pop! Zing! Yum!

Known as "lime caviar" in culinary circles, this delicious delicacy features tiny spheres of citrus juices that burst in your mouth. Those spheres are also beautiful to look at and can be yellow, green, red or pink.

First Nations people also prized this fruit and it is believed that Tamborine Mountain is a corruption of the Yugumbeh word *Jambareen* which means "Cliff of the Lime", referencing the practice of harvesting Finger Lime each year.

It is delicious when added to a Gin and Tonic at the end of a long hot day. Simply add frozen pearls (it freezes well) to the glass and make the drink as per your preference. As you drink, use your tongue to pop each sphere and savour the tangy delight as it bursts in your mouth, releasing vitamin C and folate!

In a garden the thorny shrubs provide numerous ecosystem services. It is a host for Orchard Swallowtail Butterflies and despite the caterpillars stripping leaves and leaving bare twigs, Finger Lime shrubs recover easily. It also offers refuge to small birds. They can hide amongst the thorns and even nest in the branches, protecting their young and themselves from larger predators who avoid the spikes.

Culinary applications:
- garnishes
- salads
- dukkah (after being freeze-dried)
- desserts (cheesecake! *drools*)
- seafood
- chicken
- sauces, and
- vinaigrettes.

It's no wonder that demand exceeds supply for these delightful fruits.

Flame Tree

Flame Tree
(*Brachychiton acerifolius*)

This tree from "Down Under" follows the upside-down trend with Autumn leaves in Spring.

This tree doesn't behave "normally". It keeps its thick green foliage through the colder months but then puts on a stunning display of autumnal defoliation in Spring and Summer.

The bare branches reveal the striking red flowers that give the tree its common name and a place in many gardens as a feature. The flames of red through the lush Spring greenery is a conspicuous spectacle.

The red flowers are followed by seed pods which take six months to turn brown and ripen. The pods are filled with irritating hairs that need to be harvested carefully. These hairs can cause skin or eye problems, and if inhaled can cause respiratory issues.

First Nations people developed harvesting techniques to avoid the irritating hairs and toxins in the seeds. They accomplished both feats by roasting the seeds on an open fire and eating them as a toasted snack.

After roasting to remove the toxins, the seeds can be ground to make a coffee substitute or tasty biscuits.

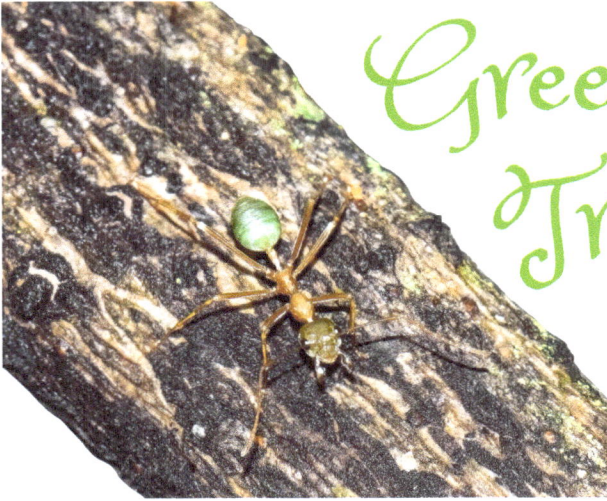

Green Tree Ants
(*Oecophylla smaragdina*)

Harvest this bush tucker with care!

These guys sting and it hurts! Interestingly, there is a theory that the intensity of the sting is related to the species of tree they choose to nest in.

They were harvested for thousands of years by First Nations people for their abdomens which taste a little citrusy, a little sweet and a little like coriander (cilantro).

Sometimes the ants would be left to ferment in water and consumed as a cough medicine and to relieve headaches and sore throats.

They create amazing aboreal nests, as featured in the photo above, that protect, not only the ants but the larvae of the Moth Butterfly (*Liphyra brassolis*) which feeds on ant eggs, larvae and pupae.

One harvesting technique involves drowning the nest in water to extract the ants without being bitten.

The nutritional profile is impressive:
- protein
- vitamin C
- iron
- amino acids
- zinc
- magnesium, and
- high levels of vitamin B12.

Happy Wanderer
(*Hardenbergia violacea*)

Not just a wandering garden feature!

This lovely vine clambers and wanders over anything in its path. It makes a great groundcover or climber with stunning purple flowers just before the end of winter.

First Nations people recognised these flowers as a "seasonal indicator" that certain types of fish could be sustainably fished from creeks.

Apparently, the tea is similar to green tea in flavour and was used in some communities, unsweetened, as a punishment for children who skipped school!

It has many other uses, including:

- adding the flowers to tea as a sweetener
- brewing a tea from the leaves (if cooled and sweetened with native honey, apparently it tastes like Sarsparilla)
- treating mouth ulcers
- treating chest complaints
- treating stomach cramps
- eating flowers to detox and cleanse
- weaving the vine to create fishnets and traps
- weaving the vine to create ropes, and
- making a dye from the flowers.

Lemon Myrtle
(*Backhousia citriodora*)

Lemon scent and flavour like no other!

If you live in a tropical or subtropical climate this is a great tree to grow with many uses and a delightful aroma.

Wait until it flowers and you smell the tiny, fluffy honey blooms! The pollinators in your garden will certainly be waiting to harvest the nectar and pollen!

It's been used by Indigenous Australians for thousands of years to treat:
- cold and flu symptoms (chew the leaves)
- stomach ulcers (tisane)
- skin conditions (leaf rub)

Lemon Myrtle has the highest level of citral (the active ingredient in citrus plants) of any plant tested. This gives it antimicrobial, antioxidant and antifungal properties. Nutritionally, the leaves are high in calcium, folate, vitamins A and E.

Commercially, it's used in soaps, lotions and cleaning products. Fresh or dried leaves add extra flavor to chicken, fish, shortbread and cheesecakes. Fresh leaves also make a lovely hot or iced tea.

The dried leaves can be added to crumbs for delicious chicken nuggets or fish, especially when fried using Lemon Myrtle Infused Olive Oil.

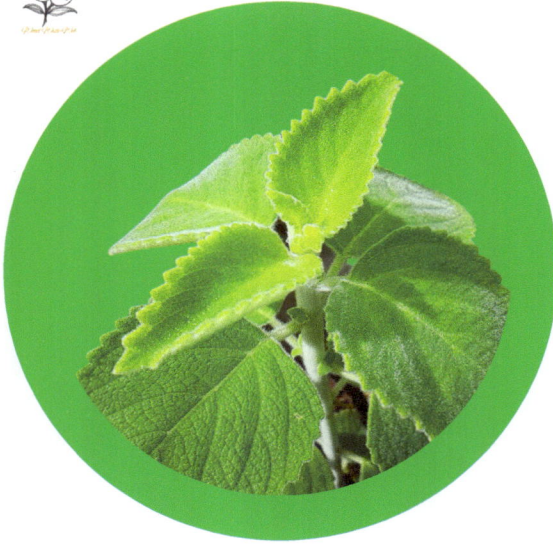

Lemon Sherbet Coleus
(*Coleus bellus*)

A perfect addition to a sensory garden!

This plant is so recently discovered that it didn't even have a proper scientific name until 2020.
I started calling it Lemon Sherbet Coleus and some have taken up that moniker.

Why Lemon Sherbet? Because if you so much as brush a leaf, the air instantly smells like Lemon Sherbet! I have found references to using this one to flavour desserts and syrups, but I can't confirm it is edible.

Another common name becoming associated with this species is Lemon Leaf Coleus.

I purchased it as Plectranthus "Mount Carbine" while it was awaiting formal status as a described plant. Most Australian Plectranthus species have since been reclassified as Coleus. Mount Carbine is in North Queensland and its rocky slopes are the only known location for this plant.

Some sources suggest it may have medicinal value, but it's a pleasure to grow just for the scent!

23

Lemon Tea Tree
(*Leptospermum petersonii*)

Make tea and keep insects away with the same plant!

Not only does this species make a delicious lemon tea, it can also be rubbed on the skin to repel insects. Of course, if you can extract the essential oil (antiseptic, antifungal and antibacterial) it will be more powerful still!

Lemon Tea Tree has a long history of medicinal use among First Nations people and was often used to boost immunity.

A research study published in 2020 highlights its efficacy as a food preservative and concludes that the results confirm the medicinal value of this plant.

Its natural distribution includes New South Wales and Queensland near wet eucalypt forests. Now you are more likely to find it in gardens or street landscapes where t is a popular ornamental species.

Lemon Tea Tree can grow to four metres, but responds well to pruning making it a lovely drought-tolerant and frost-hardy screening hedge that will feed honeyeaters and pollinators alike. The clouds of tiny white flowers feature little cups so full of nectar you can see the liquid!

In the kitchen, with a flavour profile more intense than the similar Lemon Myrtle, it can be used in baking, broths and seafood dishes. If nothing else, use it to clean your kitchen benches!

24

Mat Grasses

Mat Grasses
(*Lomandra sp.*)

This Australian plant species grows in all the Eastern Australian states as well as South Australia. It is an incredibly versatile and hardy plant that can be seen in many landscaped gardens in cities as well as in bushland.

Mat Grasses are easy to grow, tolerating a wide range of soil types and climates. It does need water to become established but provided it has enough soil depth for its substantial root system it is very drought tolerant.

Mat Rushes are a great plant species to use in areas that are vulnerable to erosion, as they hold soil well and can be used to rehabilitate creek banks. They look great in grass gardens, rockeries and make a great edging plant or gap filler.

The glossy green leaves can grow up to a metre long giving them a spiky appearance. The highly ornamental flower and seed heads appear in warmer weather and last until the weather cools.

Mat Rushes were used extensively by First Nations people over tens of thousands of years for many applications including:

- food (seeds are soaked, ground and baked into bread or added to other seeds and nuts to create a nutritious paste)
- fishing nets (the long stems are woven)
- dilly bags (carry bags), and
- mats (by drying and weaving the long stems).

Midyim Berry
(*Austromyrtus dulcis*)

Forget blueberries and grow this native superfood instead!

"*These are the most agreeable native fruit I have tasted in Australia; They are produced so abundantly as to afford an important article of food to the Aborigines...*" *James Backhouse, naturalist, 1843*

With more antioxidants than blueberries, as well as numerous vitamins and minerals, the Midyim Berry has been hailed as yet another Australian native superfood.

The delightfully delicate flowers are replaced by blueberry-sized berries that are white and speckled with tiny blue spots. The burst of flavour is also reminiscent of blueberries, but there's a tinge of eucalyptus there to remind you that it's Australian.

The plants themselves have lovely deep green leaves and coopery coloured new growth. The bushes love a good dose of sunlight and well-drained soil.

It's the perfect feature plant that yields a delicious harvest.

Native Dracaena

Native Dracaena
(*Pleomele angustifolia*)

Not just an indoor plant!

This tropical plant is found growing wild in the understorey of rainforests in Australia and South-east Asia.

In the Northern Territory of Australia it is known as Native Happy Plant.

Very young leaves are cooked and eaten with rice in some parts of South East Asia.

In India, the leaves are pounded and mixed with water. The resulting green juice is extracted to colour a dish made with glutinous rice.

The bright orange fruits can be roasted and eaten as a snack.

The seeds have a peppery taste, but the flavour tends to be insipid and lacks the spicy pungency of most pepper varieties.

As a medicinal plant, the green juice from boiled leaves is given to people suffering from asthma or shortness of breath. This green juice is also used to stimulate appetite and facilitate weight gain.

Perhaps the most exciting thing about this bush tucker plant is that it can be grown in the shade or as an indoor plant and still produce pleasantly fragranced flowers and edible fruits. To add to its appeal as an indoor plant, it has also been cultivated to produce variegated forms to suit any decor.

Native Elderberry
(*Sambucus australisica*)

An Australian elderberry perfect for pies and crumbles!

The berries of this Australian native are yellow, but culinary uses align with the black berries and flowers of its European cousin.

While evidence of use by First Nations people is difficult to find, it's safe to assume that it was consumed and perhaps used as a remedy for cold and flu symptoms.

One day I was weeding enthusiastically and talking to my son. In triumph, I pulled a huge weed! My triumph dissolved in a second, I had accidentally pulled out my Native Elderberry. I replanted and watered with seaweed solution. It survived. Phew! This plant is tough!

Native Elderberry flowers and fruits continuously for months at a time, usually from February to July. A single tree yields handfuls of ripe berries each day. Fruit can be tart, sweet or bitter depending on specific environmental conditions.

The fruit loses little texture or taste from freezing offering the option of freezing these handfuls to be used later in culinary applications that require a greater quantity of berries than those available on any given day.

The berries can be used to make
- wines,
- cordials,
- jams,
- dessert crumbles,
- pies,
- a syrup.

The syrup reportedly reduces the length and severity of cold and flu symptoms.

The flowers are also edible raw or cooked.

A note for caution: berries from plants in this genus (but not this particular species) have been known to cause stomach upsets in some individuals. Any toxins are thought to be removed by cooking.

Native Grape Vine
(*Tetrastigma nitens*)

Cut this vine for freshwater on the go!

Also known as Three Leaved Water Vine, this plant can be cut to release fresh water. Thick woody sections of the vine have been used this way for thousands of years by First Nations people. Plant purified water—who knew?!

It is a dioecious plant, meaning that there are male and female vines and both are needed for the female plant to bear fruit.

As a rainforest plant, it will grow in the shade and can also be grown as an indoor plant. Another common name is Shiny-leaved Grape referencing its attractive foliage.

The fruits, which look like a bunch of grapes, contain between 1 and 3 seeds. They are ripe when they turn completely black. The flavour is not unpleasant, but not particularly tasty either. Breaking the fruits open releases a scent like newly cut grass. Some sources indicate that cooking can improve the flavour.

They can be consumed fresh or used to make:
- jams
- preserves
- chutneys
- wine, or
- sultanas.

The leaves are also said to be edible when cooked, much like traditional grape vines.

Native Hibiscus
(*Hibiscus heterophyllus*)

Stunning, wafer thin delicate edible flowers.

This lovely Australian native grows along the East Coast. Flowers are generally white in the South and yellow in the North. The flowers only last one day, but they are tough enough to blow around in a strong wind.

As with any edible plant, there is cause for caution, though. This species is not recommended for consumption by people with kidney conditions. This recommendation is based on a single case publicised in the mid-1990s and reinforced by the lore of First Nations people who used Native Hibiscus medicinally for thousands of years.

Historical and Modern uses are similar to other Hibiscus species and include:

- petals — tea, salads
- buds — jams, salads, boiled
- whole flowers — stuffed and baked
- medicinal use.

The fibrous bark and stems of the Native Hibiscus were also used extensively by First Nations people to create items such as:

- bowstrings
- dilly bags (traditional carry bags)
- twine
- hunting nets, and
- rope.

Native Lemongrass
(*Cymbopogon ambiguus*)

Anti-inflammatory grass for warm temperate, subtropical and tropical climates.

The seed heads of this lemon grass are beautifully fluffy and ornamental while the smell is refreshing and brings a spring to one's step!

First Nations people consumed this grass as a tisane, reportedly treating coughs, colds and flus. It also has a reputation as an anti-inflammatory pain reliever.

It can be substituted for the Asian species of Lemongrass to make delicious curries and other oriental treats.

Just over ten years ago, researchers at Griffith University looked at 30 plant species used as natural medicine by Indigenous Australians.

This species of Native Lemongrass was found to be "as good as aspirin" for headaches and treating inflammation! According to Dr. Grice, the most effective way to consume it is after infusing in boiling water. I drink it as a tea and it's no chore! It's lovely hot or iced!

The tisane is becoming more commercially available taking all the work out of reaping the benefits of this amazing grass.

Native Mulberry
(*Pipturus argenteus*)

Want biodiversity? Plant Native Mulberry!

My children are regularly drawn to the tree to gather and gobble the tiny sweet fruits or search for caterpillars and eggs. They are inevitably rewarded for their efforts.

First described during Captain James Cook's 1769 voyage, this plant had already been used for centuries by various First Nations people around the Pacific region.

First Nation women and newborn babies ate the seeds. It was used medicinally to treat ailments including coughs, malaria, burns and centipede bites.

Fishing nets and dyes were created from the tough, fibrous bark. In Samoa the bark was also a key component of traditional mats.

The wood was prized for its versatility and elasticity leading to its use in the construction of dwellings around the Pacific.

It also boasts significant ecosystem services. A few moments of close observation reveals species galore. From the Eastern Sedge Frogs to Rainbow Lorikeets to countless insects, this plant brings with it much more than an edible berry!

32

Native Oregano

Native Oregano
(*Prostanthera rotundifolia*)

Whether you call it Native Mint or Native Oregano, you'll call it delicious in butter!

This pretty purple-flowering short-lived shrub is packed with volatile oils that are antibacterial, antifungal and anti-inflammatory.

First Nations people used it to treat headaches and colds.

The pungent smell is released at the slightest brush of the foliage making it an excellent choice for pathways or sensory gardens, particularly for areas children access, as the foliage and the flowers are both edible.

The flavour is unique dominated by earthier oregano, but partnered with menthol and citrus notes.

Like traditional Mediterranean oregano used around the world, it partners well with eggplant dishes and red meats.

Fresh leaves chopped and mixed into butter make a delicious addition to warm crusty bread or vegetables.

Have you noticed how many edible Australian plants have menthol and eucalyptus in their flavour profile? The taste of home...

Native Thyme

Native Thyme
(*Prostanthera incisa*)

Pretty and potent, Native Australian Thyme is the perfect native herb for savoury and sweet dishes.

It is a short-lived shrub but strikes easily from semi-hardwood cuttings. Be sure to keep it in soil that drains well. Despite its preference for regular watering, Native Thyme is susceptible to root rot.

This shrub grows well in the ground or in a pot and responds well to regular pruning.

Native Thyme was used medicinally for digestive, respiratory and skin conditions by First Nations people for thousands of years but now you're more likely to find it in the kitchen.

Warndu, a company that specialises in bush tucker catering, lists this as their favourite local Australian herb and for good reason!

The leaves contain a potent essential oil and have antifungal properties, vitamins C and A, iron and manganese.

Crushing the leaves fills the air with a minty menthol aroma that stimulates and awakens. They can be used dried or fresh, as a thyme substitute, a tisane or in natural pest control and cleaning products.

It's perfect for lamb and pork dishes or used sparingly in desserts.

A little bit goes a long way!

Native Violet
(*Viola banksii*)

Our very own violet-studded no-mow lawn for shady areas.

First described in 1770 at Botany Bay, Native Violets were likely used by First Nations people for tens of thousands of years before that.

This plant is a wonderful edible groundcover that even tolerates light foot traffic. It's a great species to plant on the steps of rockery gardens as a perfect no-mow green edible delight!

The native bees love it, and various small reptiles use it as habitat. The leaves die off during dry spells but the hardy rootstock survives and the leaves reappear with rainfall.

There are no known medicinal uses but the kidney-shaped leaves might indicate some if you follow the Doctrine of Signatures!

Many *Viola* species have edible flowers that are high in antioxidants so it's likely that this species is similarly beneficial.

To keep it in top condition for harvest, it prefers part shade or dappled shade and regular watering.

Edible flowers are a fantastic way to brighten up a salad or baking, and these delicate delights are perfect! This species flowers all year round in warmer climates.

Peanut Tree

Peanut Tree
(*Sterculia quadrifolia*)

Roast the seeds for a tasty snack!

Peanut Trees belong to the same family as Hibiscus and Cacao, but the roasted seeds taste like peanuts, which are from a different family altogether. This rainforest tree can be found in Northern Australia, Papua New Guinea and Timor.

The leaves were used medicinally by First Nations people to treat wounds and stings, while the bark was harvested for fibrecraft.

The Girringun People of the "Cassowary Coast" call this plant, *Guwala*. They ate the seeds and the roots of young trees.

The semi-deciduous nature of this tree is handy in a permaculture garden position that needs summer shade and winter sun.

The seed pods are a beautiful bright orange and contain black seeds which can be roasted to enhance flavour. After roasting they can be consumed as a snack or added to dishes as a peanut substitute. The roots of young trees are roasted before consumption.

Some sources advocate eating the seeds raw, but others warn that they contain cyclopropenoid fatty acids which are potentially harmful but will degrade if heated making them safer to consume.

Pepperberry
(*Tasmannia lanceolata*)

Versatile and vibrant on the palate, you won't find a more intriguing pepper!

Pepperberry grows in cold climates and can survive subzero temperatures. It has been used by First Nations people for thousands of years, both as a condiment and medicinally to treat venereal diseases, colic and skin complaints.

In the kitchen, it can serve as a substitute for black peppercorns, but its unique fruity flavour also makes it perfect for desserts and baking.

To my palate, it's a cross between black pepper, sweet chilli and spicy chilli flavours. It's delicious!

The leaves are also edible and can be dried and used as a less potent pepper substitute.

Don't stop there!

Even the pretty white flowers can be used to give a light peppery twist to salads.

When combined with the leaves of a native salt bush, these berries create a unique, truly Australian seasoning!

37

Queensland Nutmeg

Queensland Nutmeg (and Mace)
(*Myristica insipida*)

Our very own Nutmeg and Mace!

Related to the "true" Nutmeg, this nutmeg is a little less pungent but can be used the same way. The red aril is a native Mace, that rare spice similarly accompanying "true" Nutmeg.

This stunning rainforest tree is visited by Metallic Starlings (*Aplonis metallica*) in a gregarious, noisy mob. They harvest the aril with gusto and discard the seeds which can be ground into spice, so if you collect your native nutmeg from the ground under Starling nests you will miss out on the native mace.

First Nations people used the gum from the bark to treat ringworm and the seeds, which are high in antioxidants, are useful for dental health, improved mood and better sleep.

Trees in this genus can be confused with Laurels and Custard Apples, but the *Myristica* species bleed red sap when scratched.

Nutmeg from any plant in the *Myristica* genus must be used in moderation as high doses are toxic and at the very least may cause hallucinations.

Rain Cherry

Rain Cherry
(*Syzygium fibrosum*)

Apricot Satinash, Rain Cherry, Small Red Bush Apple, Fibrous Satinash — it's all the same bush tucker!

So many common names for a plant not commonly known! This beauty grows in the rainforest understorey across Northern Australia and in Papua New Guinea and Indonesia.

I was introduced to it by a person who descends from the original custodians of this sunburnt country.

The fruit is pleasantly crisp and tart - very refreshing on a hot day.

These small tart fruits have been eaten for thousands of years and included in jams, tarts, sauces and chutneys more recently.

It is a member of the Lilly Pilly family and has similar hedging and screening potential though it seems less popular than some other varieties. This is perhaps due to its tropical distribution.

It provides good ecosystem services with the cream to yellow flowers attracting insect and bird pollinators. Birds also enjoy the abundant fruit.

Red Back Ginger
(*Alipinia caerulea*)

Ginger from the tropical rainforest.

This classic understorey plant grows in subtropical and tropical rainforests beneath the canopy.

The root can be used in the same way as traditional ginger or chewed raw. It also produces edible bright blue berries.

The whole fruit can be dried and ground and used as a spice. Tender new shoots can be used to add a mild ginger flavour to dishes. Larger leaves may be used to wraps meats or fish before baking.

Leaves and stems were used in craftwork in pre-colonial Australia.

Fancy a sour flavour and red colouring for your herbal tea? Pop the whole fruit in the infusion!

A study conducted in 2012 found that a component in the berries may be useful in cancer treatments.

First Nations people ate the lemon-ginger flavoured berries after discarding the seeds, to activate saliva and moisten the mouth when on walkabout. According to local folklore, discarded seeds helped to establish tracks for others to follow.

This is a beautiful useful plant that also attracts buzz pollinators, such as Blue-banded Bees and Teddy Bear Bees!

Riberry

Riberry
(*Syzygium leuhmanii*)

A crimson delight from the clove family!

The berries of this lovely tree pack a true nutritional punch and have been used as food source and medicine for thousands of years by First Nations people.

They are high in folate, manganese and calcium, as well as containing high levels of the antioxidant, anthocyanin, which is thought to improve cognitive function and help prevent certain cancers, heart disease and Alzheimer's.

It was one of the first edible species to be recorded by Captain Cook in 1770 and was used by colonists to create cordials and jams.

It is now eaten raw or used to create:
- chutneys
- sauces
- jams
- desserts, and
- salads.

The spicy, honey flavour of the berries complements most meats, especially game.

This most palatable example from the Lilly Pilly family can even be used to create delicious beverages like Lilly Pilly Gin.

Its relationship with the clove family is easiest to access by drying the fruit and using it as a spice that is reminiscent of cloves and cinnamon.

River Mint (Mentha australis)

Peppermint plus spearmint plus a touch of pepper!

In the more temperate inland regions of Australia, along river banks and in wetlands, lives a minty pleasure used for tens of thousands of years by First Nations people.

River Mint was used to flavour food, repel insects and as a medicine to treat fevers, headaches and digestive disorders.

It is a perfect substitute for exotic mint species and it can be used in all the same ways, including as a tisane to relieve cough and cold symptoms.

River Mint reportedly holds aroma and flavour well when dried.

Recent research suggests that it has many beneficial components including antioxidants and phenols that may have an anti-inflammatory action on the body.

It loves regular watering and will grow in sun or shade. Be aware though, that it is susceptible to fungal infections so too much humidity can destroy the whole plant.

River Mint will grow rampantly like most mints unless it is confined to a pot.

If it does get away, it's a perfect excuse to cut it all back and make a delicious mint tisane for relief in hot weather!

Russell River Finger Lime

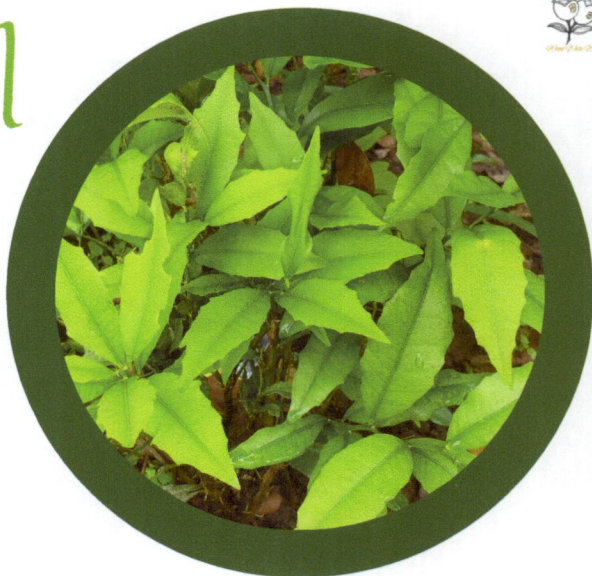

Russell River Finger Lime
(*Citrus inadora*)

Tropical lime in tiny greenish yellow packages.

This plant is rare and has a very limited natural distribution. Most people have never heard of it unless they live in the area where it is naturally found.

Unlike other Finger Lime species, it sports lush broad leaves to conceal its spikes and tiny fruit that is shaped less like a finger and more like an egg. The finger limes are smaller but sweeter than other species.

Once established it is reportedly drought hardy and will tolerate poor soils.

There is little information available on traditional uses, but it's safe to assume that First Nations people enjoyed the fruit at least for eating.

Under the Nature Conservation Act 1992, it is listed as "Vulnerable to Extinction" based on its limited natural distribution and the impact of agricultural development in its native range.

It's a citrus for collectors and rare-plant enthusiasts and thank goodness for that! Perhaps if it gains in popularity we can find out more about it.

Scrambling Lily

Scrambling Lily
(*Geitonoplesium cymosum*)

An Australian bush alternative to Asparagus.

In a genus all of its own, Scrambling Lily is truly unique. It can climb metres into the canopy but more often scrambles over the ground, small trees and logs in the understorey.

My favourite part of this plant is the flowers in bud. The teardrop shapes hang with ultimate elegance amongst the lush green foliage, before demurely opening to reveal tiny white lilies.

After my beloved grandmother's funeral, I came across some in bushland and now they always remind me of her beauty, kindness and elegance.

The fresh new shoots can be cooked and eaten and are reminiscent of Asparagus.

This climber and scrambler can be grown in any part of the garden, but prefers shade. It poses no threat to any plants it might climb or scramble over.

It is native to Eastern Australia as well as islands in the Pacific Region. With such a broad distribution, it demonstrates the ability to grow in many different climates.

Scrambling Lily produces berries that can be eaten when they are black and ripe. To me, they taste like grass, but I'm sure they would be better than nothing if I was lost in the bush!

44

Scurvy Weed

Scurvy Weed
(*Commelina sp.*)

A commelina by any other name...

This is a controversial plant in Australia, due to conflicting scientific names. While the rest of Australia calls this plant *Commelina cyanea,* the Queensland Herbarium calls it *Commelina diffusa.*

First Nations people have used plants in the *Commelina* genus as a green vegetable for thousands of years.

When Captain James Cook charted Australia's East Coast in 1770, his sailors were encouraged to eat this plant to prevent Scurvy due to its high levels of Vitamin C. It also boasts niacin, riboflavin and calcium in its nutrient profile.

It can be eaten raw or cooked, though cooking destroys the Vitamin C content. It can be used as a substitute for baby spinach.

The delightful blooms last only a few hours, giving it a common name of Dayflower, but the plant offers shelter and food to a wide variety of wildlife.

It can be used in:
- soups
- smoothies
- salads
- stews
- stir-fries, and
- sweet dishes (flowers are sweeter than leaves).

Some people also use the flowers to create a blue dye.

Sea Hibiscus
(*Hibiscus tillaceus*)

Pick lettuce from the trees in the tropics!

It grows in coastal sandy saline soils where most trees do not survive. It can also be hedged.

The other wonderful thing about this hibiscus is that it changes colour during the day. In the morning the blooms are bright yellow, but by afternoon they are a deep maroon!

The petals of the flowers and the new leaves can be used as a lettuce substitute in salads, as a garnish, boiled or fried. The roots can also be eaten if cooked.

Used by First Nations people around the Pacific for thousands of years, this bush food can also be found on tropical beaches around the world. In fact, it has been used for more than just food, with the bark being peeled in thin strips to make a fishing line. The bark was also used to make nets and various other useful fibre-based containers.

The strong timber was used in the construction of seacraft, wood carvings and for firewood.

In Indonesia the leaves are a key component in the fermenting whole soybeans to create the plant-based protein known as *Tempeh.*

46

Slender Mint
(*Mentha diemenica*)

Tiny but tough and frost tolerant too!

Australia actually has a number of mint species. They were used in the early days of colonisation but abandoned when exotic species were brought in. Of course, they had been used by First Nations people for tens of thousands of years before that.

Slender Mint can be used like any other popular mint species and has antioxidant properties with the bonus of being frost-hardy! Once established it is also drought tolerant, dying back to rootstock and returning with the rain.

This tiny mint species is invasive! It quickly spreads into lawns but then supplies a beautiful aroma that fills the air when it is crushed underfoot. It is moderately tolerant of foot traffic making it a great no-mow option.

Like most of the exotic mint species it needs regular watering to thrive. Under a garden tap is a great place to plant any moisture-loving mint.

This amazing herb was studied in 2017 as a potential component of treatment for Alzheimer's disease.

47

Sugarbag Honey

This honey won't rot your teeth!

Retailing for 200–500 Australian dollars per kilogram, this isn't the kind of honey you waste.

It was a delicacy long before Australia was colonised by the British.

First Nations people have always claimed that this honey has special properties and now science has solid evidence to back up the claims.

Sugarbag Honey has anti-bacterial properties in addition to its special sugars. These properties are similar to those found in Manuka Honey.

It contains trehalulose, a complex sugar that benefits people with diabetes because it is absorbed slowly preventing a spike in blood sugar. It also doesn't cause tooth decay! The transformation from sucrose found in nectar to trehalulose happens in the bee's gut.

Sugarbag Honey is made by stingless bees from the *Tetragonula* and *Austroplebia* genuses which live in Australia's warmer climates.

Why is it so expensive?

Primarily because beekeepers can only harvest a maximum of one kilogram per year! Experimentation and cultivation is ongoing.

Thyme Honey Myrtle
(*Melaleuca thymifolia*)

Forget the Thyme and go for the Honey!

The small leaves that cover this variable shrub give it the common common name (Thyme) and its scientific name (thymifolia or leaves that are like thyme).

It is testament to the attractiveness of this shrub that it has already been cultivated to produce commercial varieties with different coloured flowers. The names given to those cultivars are proof of its ability to blend seamlessly into mainstream gardens:

- Cotton Candy
- Little Beauty
- Pink Lace, and
- White Lace.

The Thyme-like leaves have a medicinal value like most melaleucas. The essential oil can be used as an antiseptic with antibacterial, antifungal, antiparasitic and antiviral properties.

It is the flowers that are of most interest in terms of edibility, however. They are a rich source of nectar beloved by pollinators, insects and birds alike, but were also used by First Nations people for thousands of years.

Flowers can be simply sucked for a sugar hit or stirred into fresh water to make a truly Australian sweet "lemonade".

Wait-a-while Vine

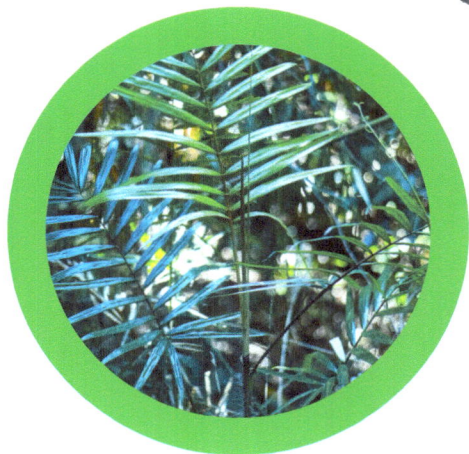

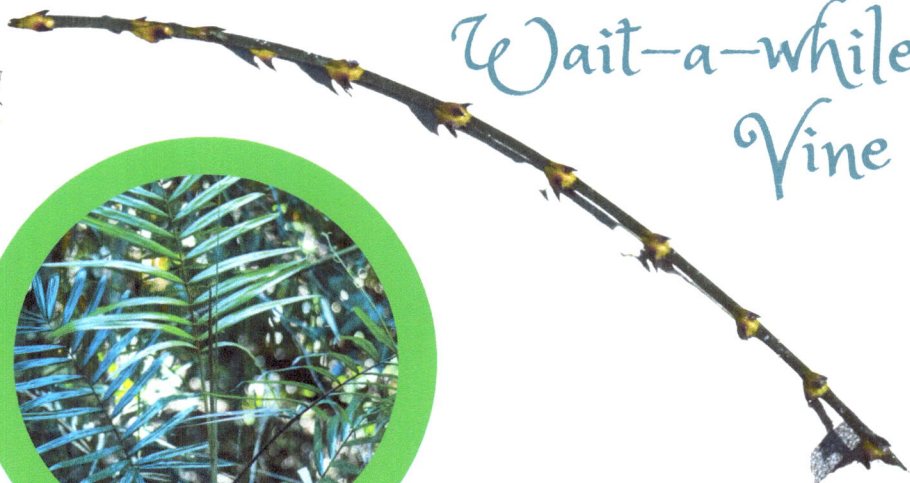

Wait-a-while Vine
(*Calamus australis*)

It's not the edible berries that will make you Wait-a-while in the jungle.

This palm, also known as Lawyer Cane, has scary spikes on long whips up to 3 meters. The whips hang down across pathways and disturbed areas. The spikes are angled backward and if you don't stop and carefully pull them out the right way, your skin will rip and tear leaving long scratches.

Those spiky whips have their uses, however. First Nations people used them to fish for freshwater prawns. The canes reportedly contain drinkable water and could be used to construct fish and animal traps.

The scaly orange berries have a soft, sweet pulp eaten by First Nations people for hundreds of years. A local boy also told me that his Aboriginal mother harvests it for "greens" when they camp in the rainforest.

It makes one wonder how much knowledge is still out there "undiscovered" by mainstream Australia.

If you go walking in the Far North Queensland rainforest, keep a keen eye out to avoid the sharp menace of Wait-a-while! Even a casual lift of the hand to brush aside foliage can mean a lengthy disentanglement.

Warrigal Greens
(*Tetragonia tetragonioides*)

A coastal Spinach alternative that grows along coastlines and in estuaries throughout the Pacific Region.

Once this spinach substitute gets going, it really gets going! It's a coastal plant that needs to be blanched or soaked to remove oxalates before consumption, then it is versatile and nutritious.
The leaves are an excellent source of Vitamin K, Vitamin C and Manganese.

In one study this salty plant showed an anti-obesity effect and it's also been used to combat gastrointestinal diabetes.

Like many coastal plants it has high tolerance of salt and a slightly salty flavour.

After harvesting the young leaves, either blanch in boiling water for one minute or soak in cold water for an hour. At this point the leaves can be used:
- in salads
- in pestos
- as a spinach alternative
- in stir-fries, and
- in pies or savoury tarts.

Used extensively by the New Zealand Maori people, it is also known as "New Zealand Spinach". It is a little odd then that there are few records of use by First Nations people in Australia. Regardless, it is likely that it has been consumed on the Australian continent for tens of thousands of years.

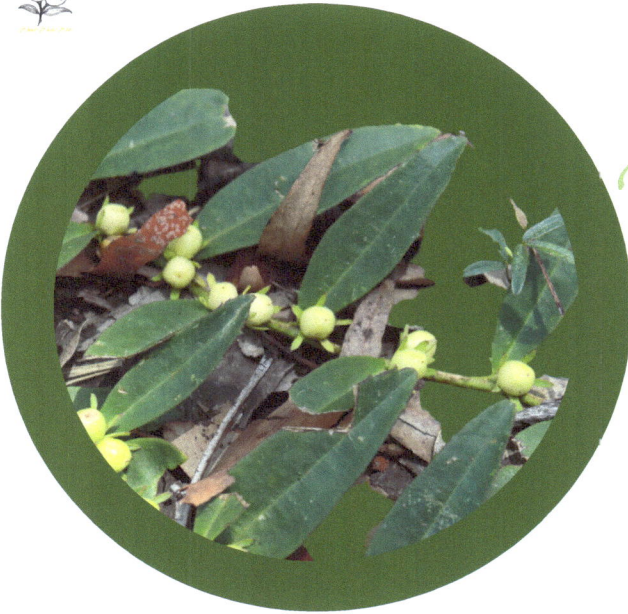

Winter Apple
(*Eremophilia debilis*)

An edible groundcover with crispy fruit.

Its scientific name can be roughly translated as "desert loving" referring to its ability to survive arid conditions, but rain during the fruiting season will result in sweeter fruit.

First Nations people ate this as a snack, discarding the large seed which fills most of the capsule. Some sources say that the fruit contains a liver enzyme and recommend moderate consumption only.

It's a lovely dense groundcover and a single plant can cover up to two square metres.

Flowers can be blue, white or pink and are star shaped. In South East Queensland the pink flowering variety can be observed in the areas around the Albert River. This colour is said to be rarer than white and blue.

It flowers sporadically throughout the year and fruits inevitably follow as green, then white, and finally a pink blush when they are ripe "Winter Apples".

Wombat Berry

Wombat Berry
(*Eustrephus latifolius*)

A coconut berry with an apple tuber.

This non-invasive climber has a lovely scrambling habit and produces attractive orange berries. Inside each berry is a small white aril which tastes like coconut. This aril was eaten by First Nations people, but the more substantial tuber was the true harvest.

The tubers were an important food source for many animals. As the name suggests, Wombats enjoy the tubers, but so do bandicoots, bettongs and other ground-dwelling marsupials.

The berries are popular with parrots, especially Australian King Parrots.

Alone in its genus, this plant is most closely related to the similarly unique Scrambling Lily.

Nineteenth Century European botanist Baron von Mueller identified this plant as being suitable for cultivation as a food crop. He is reportedly responsible for eucalyptus oil forests outside of Australia, so he clearly had a passion for the country's botany. Apparently he enjoyed the tubers, which taste like crisp apples when raw and potato when cooked!

From Our Backyard to Your Backyard

This is just a sample of the amazing range of bush tucker from around Australia. There is so much more out there to discover!

The best way to improve your understanding of the culinary delights in our backyard is to experience them first hand in your own backyard. Bush tucker is suitable for cultivation in any environment.

Most rainforest understorey plants can be grown indoors and many will still flower and fruit. Small balconies can be used to cultivate the many Australian native plants that grow well in pots and even to host a native bee hive. There are herb and shrub options for any size yard and of course trees if you are fortunate enough to have the space.

Best of all, Australian species are suited to Australian conditions and if you can find out what is endemic to your area, you are likely to need less time to maintain and nurture them.

Australian species also support Australian ecosystems and ,in so doing, maintain populations of native living organisms.

There are many retailers now selling bush tucker online and in store for those who don't want to grow or nurture species themselves. By making easy substitutions we can experience the wonder of this sunburnt country and support local industry at the same time.

When communities demonstrate a demand, avenues inevitably develop to create supply. By asking for bush tucker, we are not only experiencing new culinary adventures, we are also ensuring the survival of many species unique to Australia.

On the following pages, you will find a number of links to resources and books that can be used to access bush tucker products or to familiarise yourself with the bush tucker in your area. There are also various groups on social media platforms where you can post photos, ask questions or simply watch and learn from the photos and questions posted by others.

Let's create a demand to safeguard the future of our unique bush tucker!

Acknowledgements

In no particular order:

Thank you to my partner Kurt Thaggard for supporting the production of this ebook, proofreading, participating in endless discussions of the content, digging many holes for new plants and creating garden structures to indulge my passion for native flora and fauna. Without you my work would have less depth and satisfaction.

Thank you to my children, Grace and Henry, for encouraging me and indulging my need to spend hours tapping at a keyboard and shooting photos.

Thank you to my parents, Pam and Malcolm Frost, for instilling a love of the natural world and interest in other cultures through my childhood years.

Thank you to my father, David Andrews, an author in his own right, for cementing my love of writing and literature.

Thank you to my sisters, Emily Araman and Sally Burge, for your support and to Emily for giving me valuable advice from your perspective as a talented graphic designer.

Thank you to Jill Smith for donating your professional services to edit and proofread this work. And helping me to remove unnecessary exclamation points!

Thank you to Katie Michaelson and all the other Medium.com writers and readers for your consistent support and encouragement in my writing endeavours.

Thank you to the volunteers who read sample pages and completed surveys to help me polish the manuscript before publication.

Thank you to all those who have supported my social media content, writing and photography. By reacting and commenting and sharing your stories you give me hope that our world can change for the benefit of future generations.

Recommended Reading – Books

Identifying Bush Tucker Plants

1. **Bush Tucker: Australia's wild food harvest**
2. **Wild Food Plants of Australia**

- Low, T. (1989). *Bush Tucker: Australia's wild food harvest.* North Ryde: Angus & Robertson.
- Low, T. (1991). *Wild Food Plants of Australia.* Sydney: HarperCollinsPublishers

Using Bush Tucker Plants

1. **Warndu Mai: introducing native Australian ingredients to your kitchen**
2. **First Nations Food Companion: how to buy, cook, eat and grow indigenous Australian ingredients**

- Coulthard, D., & Sullivan, R. (2019). *Warndu Mai Good Food: introducing native australian ingredients to your kitchen.* Sydney: Hachette Australia.
- Coulthard, D., & Sullivan, R. (2022). *First Nations Food Companion: how to buy, cook, eat and grow Indigenous Australian Ingredients.* Crows Nest: Murdoch Books.

Cultural Plant Use by First Nations people

- Girramay, Jirrbal, Gulnay, Djiru, Nywaigi, Warrgamay, Warungnu, Gugu-badhun and Bandjin People. (2013). *Wabu Jararyu: cultural plant use by the Girringun Aboriginal Tribal Groups of Queensland.* Cardwell: Girringun Aboriginal Corporation.

Keeping Native Bees

- Coonan, G. (2020). *Keeping Australian Native Stingless Bees.* North Yorkshire: Northern Bee Books.
- Heard, T. (2021). *The Australian Native Bee Book.* Underwood: Sugarbag Bees.

Exploring the Bush and recording the Bush Tucker you find

- Peeters, P. (2020). *Take this Book for a Walk.* Nerang: Paperbark Writer.

Some Online Resources
used frequently by the author

- [Australian National Botanic Gardens Plant Information](#)

- [Australian Native Plants Society](#)

- [Kakadu Plum Company](#)

- [Warndu](#)

Online Resources by the Author

GET INTO IT

Index

Email

janegrowsgardenrooms@gmail.com

to purchase photos on various products such as t-shirts, posters, notebooks etc

Email

janegrowsgardenrooms@gmail.com

to purchase photos on various products such as t-shirts, posters, notebooks etc

Email

janegrowsgardenrooms@gmail.com

to purchase photos on various
products such as t-shirts,
posters, notebooks etc

Email

janegrowsgardenrooms@gmail.com

to purchase photos on various products such as t-shirts, posters, notebooks etc

Email

janegrowsgardenrooms@gmail.com

to purchase photos on various products such as t-shirts, posters, notebooks etc

Email

janegrowsgardenrooms@gmail.com

to purchase photos on various products such as t-shirts, posters, notebooks etc

Email

janegrowsgardenrooms@gmail.com

to purchase photos on various products such as t-shirts, posters, notebooks etc

Email

janegrowsgardenrooms@gmail.com

to purchase photos on various products such as t-shirts, posters, notebooks etc

Email

janegrowsgardenrooms@gmail.com

to purchase photos on various products such as t-shirts, posters, notebooks etc

Email

janegrowsgardenrooms@gmail.com

to purchase photos on various
products such as t-shirts,
posters, notebooks etc

Wood Wide Web